DEMON HIT LIST

DEMON HIT LIST

JOHN ECKHARDT

 Whitaker House

All Scripture quotations are taken from the King James Version (KJV) of the Holy Bible.

DELIVERANCE THESAURUS: DEMON HIT LIST

Crusaders Ministries
P.O. Box 7211
Chicago, IL 60690

ISBN: 0-88368-614-7
Printed in the United States of America
© 1995 by John Eckhardt

Whitaker House
30 Hunt Valley Circle
New Kensington, PA 15068
Visit our web site at: www.whitakerhouse.com

Library of Congress Cataloging-in-Publication Data

Eckhardt, John, 1957–
  Deliverance thesaurus: demon hit list / by John Eckhardt
     p. cm.
Includes bibliographical references.
  ISBN 0-88368-614-7 (alk. paper)
  1. Demonology—Terminology. 2. Exorcism—Terminology. I.
Title.
  BT975 .E25 2000
  235'.4'03—dc21   00-009254

2 3 4 5 6 7 8 9 10 11 12 13 / 09 08 07 06 05 04 03 02

Contents

Introduction

According to *Webster's Dictionary,* a thesaurus is a dictionary of synonyms and antonyms; any dictionary, encyclopedia, or other comprehensive reference book; a storehouse, repository, or treasury. The inspiration to write a deliverance thesaurus came partly from the use of *Roget's Thesaurus* in deliverance. This is summed up best by Win Worley in his book, *Demolishing the Hosts of Hell,* on page 61:

> Roget's Thesaurus *is a unique dictionary catalog of synonyms arranged in topical form. Because demons tend to "cluster" in family groupings, the thesaurus can be an amazingly helpful instrument to identify demons within a specific category. Commonly spirits in related "family" groups are under a ruler. In deliverance, the gift of discernment can zero in on a particular spirit. Often the Holy Spirit will give one the ruler's name. When this spirit is forced to manifest himself, his name, located in the thesaurus, becomes a tool to uncover his supportive network of demons. This will expedite deliverance and assure a clean sweep of that particular group.*
>
> *For example, if a spirit of selfishness was discerned and forced to*

*manifest itself, reference to the the-
saurus reveals his cohorts: Calcu-
lation, Self-Centeredness, Egotism,
Introversion, Narcissist, Stinginess,
and Pride. To dig even deeper, each of
these names can also be looked up to
secure a more complete identification
of various character deficiencies and
spiritual reinforcements that might be
present.*

Since identifying and uncovering demons by
name is so important in deliverance, the idea to write
a deliverance thesaurus is well overdue. Demons
congregate in "groupings," and knowing how they
link up is invaluable to the deliverance worker. This
thesaurus will help the worker to identify the names
of different spirits, and also group spirits together
that tend to "cluster" within people seeking deliverance. It will also be a handy reference book that the
deliverance worker can refer to from time to time
that will hopefully be a storehouse of information
that will help destroy the works of the Devil.

The names listed will not only be synonyms
of the most common spirits we deal with in deliverance, but also spirits that tend to group with them,
and other information that will be helpful in setting
a person free in a particular area. Names are important because they help us to identify the Enemy.
Remember that Satan is a "ruler of darkness" (see
Ephesians 6:12) and does not like to be exposed.
He and his cohorts work best when they are able to
operate in obscurity and darkness. When light and
identification come (often through a name), their
authority is broken and their work destroyed.

—JOHN ECKHARDT

Preface

What's in a Name?

And he asked him, What is thy name? And he answered,
saying, My name is Legion: for we are many.
—Mark 5:9

Some argue that we don't need to know the specific names of demons. After all, what's in a name? A name is a word or phrase that designates a person. Remember that when we are dealing with demons, we are dealing with personalities, not things. Names are what we use to identify persons. If someone shouts in a crowd, "Hey YOU! Come here!" you wouldn't know which "you" the person was calling. But if someone shouts your name in a crowd, there would be an immediate response.

Therefore, names are used to identify. Each of us receives a name at birth that will identify us for the rest of our lives. You will answer to that name thousands of times throughout life.

On the other hand, to be nameless means to be obscure or undistinguished. It means to be anonymous—that is, not recognized. Demons don't want you to recognize them. They want to be anonymous. Even though they have names, they would rather you not know it.

It is helpful sometimes to know the exact names of spirits you are dealing with, to destroy any excuse the demons have to stay. Sometimes demons try to use the excuse that their exact name was not called.

Mark 5:9 gives us a key revelation in dealing with the Enemy. Jesus commanded the spirit to identify itself by name. Once the Enemy identified himself, Jesus cast him out. This is the power of identification. Identifying the Enemy is a key to casting him out. The more believers can identify the Enemy by name, the more successful they will be in driving the Enemy out.

The name of Jesus is the name given above every name (Philippians 2:9). His name, therefore, gives us authority over every demon name. The names found in this thesaurus are all subject to the name of Jesus. Again, the emphasis is *name*—the name of Jesus versus the name of demons. Thank God for the name of Jesus, the name above every name.

Thesaurus
Listing

A

ABADDON (APOLLYON)

Destruction, destroyer; a place of destruction; the depths of hell. Works with spirits of death, hell, and the grave (Hades).

ABANDONMENT

Rejection, forsaken, *"grieved in spirit"* (Isaiah 54:6), deserted, cast away, cast aside, neglect, orphan, hurt, deep hurt, widow, orphan, unloved, outcast, unwanted, loneliness, isolation. Operates in widows, orphans, and adopted children, making them feel abandoned by loved ones.

ABDOMEN

Stomach, belly, gut. Serpentine spirits of lust and scorpion spirits of fear can lodge and operate in the stomach and lower abdomen. We sometimes lay hands on the stomach area and command them to manifest themselves and come out.

ABNORMAL

Bizarre, deviant, strange, weird, unnatural, uncommon, odd, unusual, irregular. (When demons are in operation, the result will be abnormalities; things that cannot be explained naturally are often demonic.)

ABOMINATION

Obscenity, disgrace, anathema, abhorrence, evil, curse, horror. (Homosexuality, lesbianism, idolatry, witchcraft, pride, lying, and cheating are all considered abominations in Scripture.)

ABORTION

Molech (Leviticus 20:1–5), spirits of Ammon (Amos 1:13), miscarriage, murder, premature termination of fetus. Works with adultery, death, destruction, and hatred of children.

ABSALOM

Pride, seduction, rebellion, vanity, treachery, betrayal, sedition, self-promotion, self-exaltation, self-destruction, death. Works in ministries to undermine authority (2 Samuel 15).

ABUSE

Offense, mistreatment, torment, criticism, cursing, exploitation, perversion, hurt; sexual abuse (rape, incest, molestation); mental abuse (mind control, domination); physical abuse (beaten, bruised, cruelty); religious abuse (legalism, control, guilt, shame, cults); emotional abuse (hurt, deep hurt, wounds); doormat (makes others walk all over a person); unforgiveness, bitterness, hatred (of abuser), anger, resentment, fear (of hurt, of being abused), memory recall. Break curses of abuse and cast out related spirits of abuse.

ACCIDENT

Spirits causing casualty, disaster, calamity, injury, catastrophe, mishap, misfortune, trauma. Often operates through a curse.

ACCUSATION

Satan (accuser, slanderer), Diabolos, accuser of the brethren (spirits that work through believers to accuse one another), slander, suspicion, schizophrenia, betrayal, jealousy, envy, paranoia, faultfinding, bitterness, hatred, finger-pointing, judging, false accusation.

ADDICTION

Compulsion, obsession, alcohol, drugs (illegal and prescription), nicotine, caffeine, sugar, exercise, spendthrift, food, craving. Addiction spirits lodge in the appetite, stomach, mouth, throat, taste buds, and nose. They enter through rejection and inheritance.

ADULTERY

Lust, fornication, unfaithfulness, promiscuity, immorality, harlotry, whoredom, extramarital affair, infidelity, lying, deception, carnality, backsliding. Lodges in the eyes (2 Peter 2:14); works with Jezebel (Revelation 2:20). Destruction (Proverbs 6:32), wounds, dishonor, reproach, shame, a marriage-breaking spirit. Operates through curses of lust and adultery.

AFFECTATION

Theatrics, playacting, pretension, hypocrisy. Works with schizophrenia.

AHAB

Works with Jezebel; destruction of the family priesthood; weakness in males; fear; abdication of authority; weak, irresponsible, abdicating.

AIMLESSNESS

Wandering, drifting, straying, indecision, purposeless.

ALCOHOLISM

Bacchus (god of drunkenness), drunkenness, addiction and craving for alcohol; delirium tremens, intemperance, intoxication. Works with pride (Isaiah 28), rejection, poverty (Proverbs 23:21), wounds, hurt, bruises, sorrow, contention, lust, perversion, insomnia, violence (Proverbs 23:29–35), rage, mockery (Proverbs 20:1), escape. Break all curses of alcohol and addiction.

ALLERGIES

Asthma, hay fever, respiratory problems, bronchitis; spirits operating in the sinuses and lungs. Works through curses of infirmity and inheritance.

AMMON

Incest, perversion, abortion. Entered the son of Lot and his daughter through incest (Genesis 19:30–38).

ANCESTRAL

Hereditary, maternal, paternal, genealogical, traits, ethnic, racial, family line, bloodline, roots, family tree. Ancestral and hereditary curses are the result of the sins of the fathers (Jeremiah 32:18), especially witchcraft, occultism, perversion, and idolatry.

ANGER

Animosity, choler, fury, gall, hatred, rage, resentment, temper, indignation, wrath (gives place to the Devil: Ephesians 4:26–27); violence, murder, cruelty (Genesis 49:6), bitterness, unforgiveness, retaliation, spite, revenge, outrage, hostility, enmity, foolishness. Command anger to come out of the bosom (Ecclesiastes 7:9).

ANGUISH

Suffering, torment, pain, agony, distress, affliction, heartache, grief, misery, sorrow, torture, grief, anxiety, cruelty, bondage (Exodus 6:9), dire straits.

ANIMOSITY

Hostility, enmity, contention, hatred, anger, strife, resentment, revenge, retaliation, spite, gall.

ANOREXIA NERVOSA

Eating disorder, starvation, death, fear of becoming fat, compulsive dieting, depression, self-rejection.

ANTICHRIST

A religious spirit: operates strongly in false religions; fights against Christ and the truth of the Gospel; blasphemy, false teaching, error (1 John 4:1–6).

ANTI-SEMITISM

Hatred of Jews, bigotry, prejudice, Ishmael, Nazi.

ANTI-SUBMISSIVE

Stubbornness, rebellion, disobedience, self-will, pride.

ANXIETY

Worry, apprehension, dread, fear, nervousness, panic, restlessness, uneasiness, tension, fretfulness.

APATHY

Unconcern, indifference, lethargy, passivity, coldness, detachment, insensitivity, listlessness, stoicism.

APHRODITE

Lust, perversion, sensuality, Venus, false love.

APPETITE

Spirits operating in the appetite include addiction, gluttony, lust for food, eating disorders, anorexia nervosa, bulimia, starvation, loss of appetite.

APPREHENSION

Fear, dread, anxiety, nervousness, worry, alarm, suspicion, mistrust.

ARGUMENTATIVE

Debate, dispute, contention, strife, quarrelsome, discord, disagreement.

ARRESTED DEVELOPMENT

Spirits that hinder from growing into adulthood: immaturity, hindrance, blockage, obstruction of the personality, foolishness, infantile, juvenile, adolescent; bound and blocked personality.

ARROGANCE

Rahab (Psalm 89:10), Leviathan (Job 41), pride, insolence, conceit, disdain, ego, haughtiness, high-mindedness, loftiness, self-love, self-importance, vanity, presumption, scorn, overbearing pride, pretension, exaggerated opinion of oneself.

ARTHRITIS

Enters through unforgiveness and inheritance; pain, torment.

ASHTORETH

Female deity of Baal; fertility goddess; lust, sensuality, debauchery, drunkenness.

ASTHMA

Allergies, respiratory problems.

ATHEISM

Unbelief, skepticism, doubt, humanism.

ATTENTION GETTING

Affectation, playacting, schizophrenia, rejection.

B

BAAL

Idolatry, lust, debauchery, drunkenness; name meaning lord, master possessor, owner; linked to Ashtoreth.

BACKBITING

Lying, malice, slander, gossip, criticism, abuse, strife, whispering (2 Corinthians 12:20), envy, jealousy, anger, bitterness, competition, evil speaking.

BACKLASH

Demons retaliate and attack those who attack and destroy Satan's kingdom. This is called backlash, reaction, repercussion, resentment, resistance, response, and retaliation.

BARRENNESS

Fruitless, unproductive, unrewarding, vain, useless, sterility, impotence. Barrenness is the result of a curse. Barren spirits can operate in the womb causing infertility in women.

BEELZEBUB

Lord of the flies (sovereign of evil spirits), a ruling spirit (Matthew 12:24).

BELIAL

Worthlessness, wickedness, destruction.

BETRAYAL

Deception, dishonesty, treachery, Judas Iscariot, treason, sedition, disloyalty, hypocrisy, jealousy, cruelty, rebellion, mutiny.

BIBLE

Spirits that block and hinder people from reading and understanding the Bible; debate (makes people argue the Bible); closed Bible ("I won't let him learn"); Logos ("I misquote the Bible"); spiritual blindness; tiredness (while reading the Bible); confusion (while reading the Bible); lawyers (spirits who study Scriptures for the purpose of argument and debate); hatred of the Bible, fear of the Bible, unbelief ("I don't believe the Bible"); no understanding, no revelation, darkness, veil (2 Corinthians 3:15); boredom (while reading the Word); wresting and twisting the Word (2 Peter 3:16); dogmatic (teaching and preaching of the Word); tradition (making the Word of no effect; Mark 7:13).

BITTERNESS

Unforgiveness, resentment, revenge, retaliation, root of bitterness (Hebrews 12:15), hidden bitterness, gall, wormwood, poisonous root, hard bondage (Exodus 1:14), complaining, murmuring, backbiting, envy, strife (James 3:14), wrath, anger (Ephesians 4:31), cursing (Romans 3:14), jealousy. Opens the door for sickness and infirmity.

BLASPHEMY

Cursing, heresy, impiety, profanity, sacrilege, lewdness, irreverence.

BLINDNESS

Natural and spiritual, darkness, groping, veiled, lacking vision, hidden, covered, cataracts (natural and spiritual), hardness of heart, spiritual dullness, undiscerning, ignorance, deception, Pharisee. Many religious spirits operate to keep people in the dark concerning the truth and spiritual things.

BLOCKAGE

Obstruction; spirits that block spiritual growth, finances, relationships, prayer life, study of the Word, ministry, and so on. Bar, barrier, obstacle, roadblock, wall. Spirits that impede, choke, close off, cut off, stop up, sever, deter, dam, bar, arrest, thwart. Spirits that block and obstruct revelation, answered prayer, prosperity, or church growth.

BOASTING

Pride, self-flattery, pretension, ego, arrogance, haughtiness, self-importance, exaggeration, conceit, self-applauding, vainglory, bragging, chauvinism.

BONDAGE

Slavery, servitude, subjection, yokes, chains, shackles, fetters, captivity.

BRAINWASHING

Indoctrination, mind control, cults.

BROKENHEARTED

Sorrow, grief, sadness, crying, bruised, wounded, disappointment, melancholy, dejected, depression.

BUDDHA

Idolatry, death, occultism, Eastern religions and mysticism, hopelessness, despair.

BURDENS

Heaviness, heavy burdens, anxiety, albatross, hindrance, load, sorrow, stress, care, false burdens, guilt, oppression.

C

CAMOUFLAGE

Disguise, cloak, conceal, cover up, deceive, hide; mask, masquerade, veil, smoke screen, blind, chameleon (evil spirits are good at hiding and camouflaging their work); haystack ("I'm hard to find").

CARNALITY

Fleshly, earthly; lewdness, sensuality, worldliness, lust, lasciviousness, immorality; strife, envy, division (1 Corinthians 3:3).

CHEMOSH

Idol of the Moabites meaning subduer, depressor, vanquisher, an incubus (sexual spirit that attempts intercourse with women) or succubus (sexual spirit that attempts intercourse with men), concealed, the planet Saturn.

CHRONIC

Habitual, constant, continual, deep-rooted, deep-seated, lifelong, lingering, persistent, stubborn. Chronic sicknesses and diseases, chronic financial problems, chronic marital problems, and so on. Problems and conditions that won't respond to prayer, fasting, and the Word are chronic conditions that need to be dealt with in deliverance.

CLAIRVOYANCE

Extrasensory Perception (ESP), foreknowledge, premonition, telepathy, sixth sense, divination, telekinesis. Psychic spirits often operate through inheritance.

COMPETITION

Antagonism, ambition, rivalry, strife, emulation, contention, pride, driving, argument, pride, ego, strife, rivalry, jealousy, envy, ambition.

CONDEMNATION

Guilt, accusation, blame, judgment, legalism, Pharisee, religious control, false doctrine, salvation by works, false holiness.

CONFUSION

Disorientation, chaos, mind control, befuddlement, Babel (Genesis 11), idolatry (Isaiah 41:29), sexual perversion (Leviticus 18:23), schizophrenia, insanity, madness, envy, strife (James 3:16), frustration, incoherence, forgetfulness, mix up, tailspin ("I confuse her thoroughly"), puzzle ("I mix him up").

CONSCIENCE

Spirits operating in the conscience include guilt, condemnation, evil conscience, seared conscience, hardness.

CONTENTION

Argument, strife, division, fighting, discord, confusion, envy, jealousy, pride (Proverbs 13:10); scorning (Proverbs 22:10), anger, bitterness.

CONTROL

Possessiveness, dominance, witchcraft, Jezebel, Ahab, matriarchal spirits, religious control, control from the pastor, denominational control, mind control, manipulation, intimidation, fear.

CORRUPTION

Dishonesty, extortion, fraud, depravity, immorality, impurity, perversion, vice, vulgarity, rottenness.

COVETOUSNESS

Stealing, kleptomania, materialism, greed, discontent, self-seeking, self-indulgence, avarice, lust.

CRUELTY

Spite, revenge, retaliation, malice, sadism, unmerciful, ruthless, hardhearted, coldblooded, jealousy (Song of Solomon 8:6), wrath (Genesis 49:7), murder, hatred, anger.

CULTS

Hare Krishna, Jehovah's Witnesses, Christian Science, Rosicrucianism, Theosophy, Urantia, Unity, Mormonism, Bahaism, Unitarianism; faction, party, schism, heresy, false teaching, religious spirits, control, confusion, deception, error.

CURSES

Ancestral and generational, the result of the sins of the fathers; curses of death and destruction, sickness and infirmity, lust and perversion, incest, rape, mental illness, schizophrenia, poverty, witchcraft, idolatry, destruction of the family priesthood, Ahab and Jezebel, rejection.

Signs of curses include (1) mental and/or emotional breakdown; (2) repeated or chronic sicknesses (especially if hereditary); (3) barrenness, a tendency to miscarry, or related female problems; (4) breakdown of marriage, family alienation; (5) continuing financial insufficiency; (6) being accident-prone; (7) a history of suicides and unnatural or untimely deaths (from *Blessing or Curse* by Derek Prince); (8) abuse and mistreatment from other people; (9) vagabondism and a wandering lifestyle.

Evil, misfortune, calamity, trouble, plague, affliction, torment, harm, vexation, jinx.

CURSING

Blasphemy, coarse jesting, gossip, criticism, backbiting, mockery, belittling, railing, profanity, abuse, swearing, bitterness, hatred, anger, pride.

D

DANCING

Rhythmic, sensual dancing; worldly dancing, dirty dancing, lust.

DEATH

Termination, premature death through accidents, heart attacks, strokes, cancer, sickness and disease, murder, abortion. Operates through curses of death and destruction, angel of death, Grim Reaper, black horse, king of terrors, rigor mortis, murder, deathblow, Molech, suicide, fatality, lethal. Works with hell (Revelation 20:13–14).

DEBAUCHERY

Licentiousness, whoredom, self-gratification, self-indulgence, over-indulgence, unrestraint, incontinence, revelry, drunkenness.

DEFIANCE

Resistance, rebellion, anti-submissiveness, antagonism, insubordination, disobedience.

DEJECTION

Depression, heaviness, melancholy, sadness, despair, despondency, discouragement, brokenhearted, downcast.

DESTRUCTION

Ruin, devastation, calamity. Works with pride (Proverbs 16:18), poverty (Proverbs 10:15), death (Job 28:22), misery (Romans 3:16). Also operates through generational curses (Lamentations 3:64–66).

DIVORCE

A marriage-breaking spirit; hardness of heart (Matthew 19:3–9), separation, bitterness, hurt, rejection, anger, fear of marriage, guilt, shame, condemnation.

DOCTRINAL

False doctrines and teachings of all kinds; doctrinal obsession, error, heresy, doctrines of devils, various and strange doctrines; all cults.

DOG

Doberman (vicious).

DOMINATION

Control, Jezebel, witchcraft, matriarchal spirits; control by mother, father, pastor, church; religious control, mind control, fear, intimidation.

DOUBT

Unbelief, skepticism, self-delusion.

DRAGON

Sea serpent, Leviathan (Isaiah 27:1).

DREAD

Fear, terror, Gorgon, Medusa, panic, horror, sudden fear.

DRUGS

Legal and illegal; addiction, reaction, dependency, sorcery (Greek word: *pharmakeia,* meaning drugs or sorcery; Revelation 9:21). Names same as drug (e.g., Heroin, Marijuana, and so on); rebellion, disobedience, hallucination, depressant, stimulants, narcotics, sedatives, anti-depressants, hypnotic.

E

EMOTIONS

Emotional problems, bound and blocked emotions, grief, sadness, crying, anger, hatred, rage, uncontrollable emotions, hurt. Command spirits to come out of the emotions.

EPILEPSY

Fits, convulsions, seizures.

ESCAPE

Withdrawal, passivity, sleepiness, stoicism, alcohol, drugs, silence, depression, apathy.

F

FAILURE

Curses, defeat, frustration, discouragement, suicide, depression, sorrow, confusion, rejection, sadness.

FALSE

False love, false personality, false gifts, false prophecy, false tongues, false revelation, false doctrine, false prophet, false teaching, false church, false anointing, false praise, false worship, false friendship; phony, fake, counterfeit, deception, lying, hypocrisy, Pharisee, dishonesty, flattery, pretense, false religious burdens, false responsibility.

FAMILIAR SPIRITS

Spirit guides. These spirits are familiar with the family and go from generation to generation.

FATIGUE

Tiredness, weariness, laziness.

FEAR

Of making wrong decisions, rejection, being hurt, judgment, authority, failure, man, darkness, being alone, death, witchcraft, heights, demons, deliverance, losing salvation, disapproval, accusation, being wrong, spiritual gifts, responsibility, marriage, having children, pain, sickness, confrontation, cancer, driving, insanity, heart attack, the future, crowds. Horror, panic, fright, sudden fear, terror, dread, apprehension; causes torment (1 John 4:18).

FIGHTING

Strife, violence, contention, anger, rejection, murder, hatred, rage, combative.

FILTH
Pollution, dirt, foulness; of flesh and spirit (2 Corinthians 7:1); naughtiness, wickedness (James 1:21).

FLATTERY
False praise, seduction, lying, deception.

FLIRTATION
Seduction, personality change.

FOOLISH
Senseless, irrational, crazy, silly, stupid.

FORGETFULNESS
Mind block, amnesia, memory loss, absent-mindedness.

FORTUNE-TELLING
Divination, crystal ball, palm reading, tarot cards, psychic, witchcraft.

FREEMASONRY
Masonic spirits of witchcraft, idolatry, curses, occultism, deception, bondage, control, third eye, mental confusion, spiritual apathy, emotional hardness, doubt, skepticism, unbelief, infirmities, sicknesses, allergies, destruction, financial ruin, false religion, antichrist, pride, Eastern Star.

FRIGIDITY

Coldness, marriage-breaking spirit. A spirit that blocks the sex drive and can enter through molestation or rape.

FRUSTRATION

Defeat, disappointment, anger, confusion.

G

GAMBLING

Betting, compulsion, driving, lottery, debt, poverty, mishandling money, lying, craps, snake eyes, seven-eleven, off-track betting, chance, luck.

GLOOM

Bleakness, despondency, misery, sadness, woe, darkness, dejection, melancholy.

GLUTTONY

Nervousness, idleness, self-rejection, frustration, indulgences, compulsive eating, self-pity, self-reward, addiction, obesity.

GREED

Lust, avarice, covetousness, selfishness, stinginess, gluttony. Works with uncleanness (Ephesians 4:19).

GRIEF

Misery, sadness, heartache, anguish, mourning, distress, lamentation, misfortune, adversity, loss, mishap, broken heart, ache, hurt, pain, crying, cruelty.

GUILE

Deceitfulness, fraud, deception, craftiness, sneakiness, cunning, slyness, foxiness, wiles, shrewdness.

GUILT

Condemnation, unworthiness, embarrassment, self-condemnation, cults, false doctrine. Operates strongly with religious spirits.

H

HABIT

Compulsion, addiction, lust, nicotine, alcohol, drugs, nervous habits.

HADES

Spirits of death, hell, and the grave; destruction, sheol, abyss.

HARASS

Badger, irritate, molest, pester, torment, aggravate, annoy, plague, vex.

HARDSHIP

Ordeal, test, affliction, misfortune, misery, difficulty.

HATRED

Detestation, dislike, enmity, ill will, loathing, hostility, aversion, dislike. Hatred of truth, correction, God, Scriptures, men, women, husband, wife, children, black people, white people, Jews, authority, preachers, deliverance, the church. Bitterness, murderous hate, retaliatory hate.

HAUGHTY

Proud, arrogant, overbearing. Works with destruction (Proverbs 18:12); scorning, *"proud wrath"* (Proverbs 21:24); self-importance, vanity, ego, insolence, conceit, disdain.

HEADSTRONG

Obstinate, stubborn, willful, self-will, childlike self-will, anti-submissive, rebellion, independent, unyielding, contrary.

HIDDEN INHERITANCE

Physical, emotional, or mental; curses; ancestral, maternal, paternal; lust, addictions; cultural; bitterness, anger, hatred, prejudice, ethnic pride.

HIGH-MINDEDNESS

Lofty.

HINDER

Hamper, impede, block, retard, stop, resist, thwart, obstruct, delay, slow, restrain.

HINDRANCE (Blockage and Obstruction)

Spirits that hinder, block, and obstruct: no love, no help, no friends, no success, no lodging, no pity, no understanding, no wisdom, no relief (torment), no rest, no solution, no power, no ability, no light (darkness), no healing, no deliverance, no happiness, no joy, no victory, no control, no future (hopelessness), no liberty (control), no discernment (blindness), no prosperity, no breakthrough, no direction, no name, no identity, no confidence, no peace.

No open doors (closed doors), no money (poverty), no job, no sense, no way, no value, no worth, no presence of God (Ichabod), no anointing, no blessings (curses), no communication, no growth, no order (confusion), no support, no morals, no escape, no commitment, no faithfulness, no self-control, no chance, no opportunity, no family, no transportation, no mobility, no break, no time, no room, no space, no health, no strength, no home, no satisfaction, no vision, no counsel. These spirits are also the result of curses.

HINDUISM

False religion, hopelessness (because of caste system), idolatry, confusion, reincarnation.

HOMOSEXUALITY

Perversion, uncleanness, confusion, lust, rebellion.

HORROR

Dread, foreboding, alarm, sudden fear, terror, apprehension, fright, panic.

HURT

Wound, brokenhearted, deep hurt, bruised, grief, abuse, cruelty.

HYPERACTIVITY

Restlessness, driving, pressure.

HYPOCRISY

Deceit, Pharisee, guile, lying, pretense, false love, false worship, false holiness.

I

INABILITY

To give and receive love; to communicate.

IDLENESS

Passivity, laziness, slothfulness, depression, lethargy, procrastination.

IDOLATRY
Icons, pictures, relics, Baal, covetousness.

IGNORANCE
Incomprehension, simplicity, blindness, darkness, illiteracy.

IMMORALITY
Lust, ungodliness, profanity, uncleanness.

IMPORTANCE
Pride.

IMPULSIVE
Rash, careless, hasty.

IMPURITY
Uncleanness, immodesty, pornography, adultery, lewdness.

INCEST
Spirits of Moab and Ammon. Operates through curses of incest, lust, and perversion. Taboo, illicit.

INDEPENDENCE
Self-rule, self-government, rebellion, isolation, self-protectiveness, self-sufficient, pride, rejection, fear, distrust, self-reliance.

INDIFFERENCE

Unconcern, apathy, coldness, lackadaisical, listless, insensitive.

INFECTION

Virus, poison, disease, plague, infirmity, sickness, illness.

INFIRMITY

Disease, illness, sickness, ailment (by name), affliction, any sickness or disorder.

INSANITY

Madness, confusion, lunacy, mania, delirium, deranged.

INSECURITY

Inferiority, low self-esteem, fear of what others think, self-doubt, timidity, shyness, embarrassment, self-consciousness, uncertainty.

INTELLECTUALISM

Knowledge, pride, rationalization, reasoning, philosophy.

J

JEALOUSY

Envy, suspicion, covetousness, resentment, spite, bitterness, distrust, paranoia, insecurity, schizophrenia, selfishness, hatred, bedlam.

JEHOVAH'S WITNESSES

Cult, another Jesus, another spirit, another gospel, heresy, false doctrine, error; pride; judgmental; religious spirits including deception, debate, argumentative, false prophecy, resistance to the truth.

JEZEBEL

Female dominance, rebellion, witchcraft, control, manipulation, whoredom, seduction, false doctrine, idolatry, fornication. Operates through a curse destroying God's order and the family priesthood; works with Ahab in males; name meaning untouchable, non-cohabiting, without husband, adulterous, base, licentious (2 Kings 9:22).

K

KARATE

Martial arts, witchcraft, mind control, violence, lust, rebellion, anger, murder.

KORAH

Rebellion, sedition (Numbers 16).

L

LACK

Poverty, insufficiency. Break curses of poverty and lack.

LAWLESSNESS

Rebellion, insubordination, anarchy, chaos, sedition, crime, abandon, license, unruliness, disorder, licentiousness, self-indulgence, intemperance, incontinence, disobedience, nonconformity, corruption.

LAZINESS

Idleness, slothfulness, listlessness, lethargy, sleepiness, drowsiness, comatose, passivity, heaviness, apathy, slowness, tardiness.

LEGION

Army, brigade, regiment, multitude, mass, great number, throng, division, battalion, company, troop, corps, unit, division, squad, horde, myriad, scores, drove, flock, group (Mark 5:1–20).

LETHARGY

Sluggishness, dullness, heaviness, slowness, stupor, passivity, sloth, sleepiness, apathy, indifference, laziness, listlessness, drowsiness.

LEVIATHAN

Pride, *"king over all the children of pride"* (Job 41:34). Sea monster, sea serpent, dragon, hardness of heart, vanity, conceit, ego, haughtiness, colossus, titan, giant, mammoth, mastodon, arrogance, haughtiness, stubbornness, restlessness. Large sea serpent, prophesied to be destroyed by the Lord in Isaiah 27:1. Operates through a curse (Psalm 119:21). Works with destruction (Proverbs 16:18).

LEWDNESS

Lust, lustfulness, carnality, impurity, immodesty, debauchery, self-indulgence, incontinence, sexual passion, abandon, obscenity, pornography.

LIBERTINE

Sensualist, hedonist, epicurean, playboy, swinger, free lover, adulterer, fornicator, seducer, womanizer, whoremonger, pimp, gigolo, rapist, dirty old man, pervert, flasher, bed hopper, Casanova, Don Juan, wolf, goat, dog.

LICENTIOUSNESS

Debauchery, lewdness, nymphomania, concupiscence, lust, promiscuity, lawlessness, incontinence, unrestraint.

LIEUTENANT

Assistant, aide, helper, deputy, second in command, right hand, group captain, squadron leader. (Satan has many demons that act as lieutenants under his command.)

LION

Cat, vigor, master, intrepid warrior, tiger, wildcat, ferocity, fierceness, ferociousness, viciousness. (There are many lion-like spirits in the kingdom of darkness. All Sikhs have the name *Singh,* meaning "lion"—ruling spirit is often of a lion.) (See 1 Peter 5:8.)

LISTLESSNESS

Idleness, passivity, dullness, slothfulness, lethargy, apathy, indifference, lukewarmness, laziness, inattentiveness.

LOINS

Reproductive organs, strength, potency, virility, pride in sexual ability. Command spirits of lust to come out of the loins.

LONELINESS

Isolation, alienation, withdrawal, depression, despair, discouragement, defeatism, dejection, hopelessness, suicide, death, insomnia, heaviness, disgust.

LUNACY

Insanity, madness, neurosis, hysteria, delirium, mental illness, delusion, disorientation, paranoia, mania, psychosis, derangement.

LURK

Sneak, lie low, hide, conceal oneself, lie in wait, tiptoe, prowl, ambush, creep, crouch (Psalm 10:10), stay hidden. (See Psalm 10:8.)

LUST

Sexual (see sexual spirits), materialistic, greed, ravenousness, covetousness, avarice, appetite, ambition, grasping, longing, desire, passion, craving, abuse, adultery, burning passions, concupiscence, femininity (in males), masculinity (in females), frigidity, homosexuality, lesbianism, immorality, sexual impurity, uncleanness, lasciviousness, lust of the eyes, lust of the flesh, lust for power, lust for position, lust for money, masturbation, incest, rape, lewdness, prostitution, whoredom, sodomy, incubus, succubus, pornography, voyeurism, wandering eyes, perversion, fantasy.

LYING

Hypocrisy, guile, double-dealing, dishonesty, perjury, misleading, falsehood, little white lies, big liar, deceit, exaggeration.

MACHIAVELLIAN

Machiavelli (political expediency is placed above morals; works in government).

Cunning, deception, deceit, dishonesty, double-dealing, trickery, intrigue, foxiness (Luke 13:32), Herodian, slyness, craftiness, wily, expedient, unscrupulous.

MADNESS

Insanity, mania, mental illness, neurosis, caused by oppression (Ecclesiastes 7:7), by idolatry (Jeremiah 50:38), and by a curse (Deuteronomy 28:28).

MAGIC

White magic, black magic, sorcery, divination, incantation, black arts, voodoo, wizardry, abracadabra, hocus-pocus, trickery, illusion, spell, sorcery, wizardry, charm, enchantment, black arts, necromancy, conjuring, spell.

MALICE

Hatred, animosity, hostility, anger, wrath, bitterness, unforgiveness, spite, envy, jealousy, cruelty, murder, grudge, venom, ill will, vindictiveness, enmity, meanness, malignity, animosity, resentment, viciousness (Ephesians 4:31).

MAMMON

The god of money, idolatry (Matthew 6:24). Love of money, covetousness, greed, corruption, filthy lucre, materialism.

MAMMOTH

Huge, enormous, gigantic, hippopotamus, behemoth (Job 40:15–24), leviathan (Job

41), immense, monstrous, elephant, massive.

MANIPULATION
Control, deception, deceit, lying, rejection.

MARAUDING
Raiding, roving, plundering, pillaging, preying, looting.

MARITAL
Divorce, separation, strife, division, Ahab or Jezebel (marriage-breaking spirits), witchcraft.

MARTIAL
Militant, warlike, aggressive, combative.

MARTIAL ARTS
Karate, Kung Fu, Judo, and so on; violence, anger, murder, occult, witchcraft, lust (all kinds by name).

MASQUERADE
Disguise, camouflage, pretense, imposter, deception, Mardi Gras, carnival, Halloween, mask.

MASTURBATION
Self-gratification, self-abuse, self-defilement, fantasy, lust, pornography, Onan (Genesis 38:9), self-love.

MATRIARCHAL

Female domination, Jezebel, control from mother, dominant wife, homosexuality, Ahab.

MAZE

Labyrinth, puzzle, complex, perplexity, web, bewilderment.

MAZZAROTH

Prognostication, constellations, twelve signs of the zodiac, astrology, horoscopes. (See Job 38:32.)

MEDICATION

Addiction to medication, sorcery (Greek word: *pharmakeia*), mind-altering, sleepiness, drowsiness.

MELANCHOLY

Dejection, despondency, depression, gloominess, sadness, sorrow, hopelessness, despair, defeatism, discouragement, heaviness (Isaiah 61:3), grief, sadness.

MEMORY

Memory loss, flashback, memory recall, bad memories, hurtful memories, painful memories, blocked memories, trauma, denial, Alzheimer's disease, past.

MENTAL ILLNESS

Insanity, madness, confusion, mania, retardation, senility, schizophrenia, paranoia, hallucinations.

METAPHYSICS

New Age.

MIND-BINDING

Confusion, fear of man, fear of failure.

MIND CONTROL

Octopus and squid spirits having tentacles; confusion, mental pressure, mental pain, migraine. Ask the Lord to sever the tentacles of mind control.

MIND IDOLATRY

Intellectualism, rationalization, pride, ego, pride of knowledge, philosophical spirits.

MINION

Subordinate, deputy, assistant, underling, inferior (lower-ranking spirits operating under lieutenants, captains, and rulers).

MISCARRIAGE

Premature birth (operates through curses), abortion, failure.

MISCHIEF

Trouble, misconduct, misbehavior, naughtiness; works with vanity (Psalm 10:7), boasting (Psalm 52:1), sorrow (Psalm 55:10), and witchcraft (Acts 13:8–10). (See Proverbs 4:16.)

MISERY

Suffering, woe, evil, agony, torment, distress, anguish, unhappiness, calamity, sorrow. Works with destruction (Romans 3:16).

MOAB AND AMMON

Incest, perversion (sons of Lot and his daughters through an incestuous union). (See Genesis 19.)

MOCKERY

Ridicule, taunting, scorning, derision, disdain, contempt, disrespect.

MOLECH

Idol to whom babies were sacrificed (Leviticus 18:21; 20:2–5). Abortion, child sacrifice, hatred of children, murder; name meaning "king," "ruler."

MOLESTATION

Abuse, pain, hurt, rape, sodomy, incest, violation, offense, wound, bruise, torment, mistreatment, confusion, guilt, shame, bitterness, fear, anger, hated (of abuser), mind control.

MONARCH

Tyrant, dictator, despot, overlord, ruler, king (ruling spirits often identify themselves by titles such as monarch, ruler, and so on).

MONKEY

Imp, little rascal, little devil, mischief-maker, troublemaker, fool, mime.

MONSTER

Dragon, gargoyle, griffin, sea serpent, sea monster (Leviathan; Job 41), ghoul, phantom, ghost, giant, behemoth (Job 40:15–24), ape, gorilla, mammoth, hippopotamus, Gog and Magog (Ezekiel 38), brute, incubus, succubus, horror, terror, panic, sudden fear, nightmare, Hydra, Gorgon, titan, werewolf, ogre, centaur (many Greek mythological monsters are really demons), Chimera, zombie, vampire, Medusa.

MOONSTRUCK

Madness, insanity, lunacy, dazed, hysteria.

MURDER

Hatred (1 John 3:15), homicide, bitterness, unforgiveness, anger, malice, spite, jealousy, revenge, retaliation.

MURMURING

Complaining, whispering, bitterness, faultfinding, accusation, rebellion, lust, impatience, unbelief.

MUSIC

Orpheus, Apollo, pride in musical ability. All forms (rock, jazz, blues, and so on).

Pride, vanity, idolatry of music personalities, beat, rhythm.

MYSTICISM

Occultism, esoterics, theosophy, transcendentalism, metaphysics.

N

NARCISSIST

Self-serving, selfishness, ego, conceit, vanity, pride.

NATIONALISM

Pride (of color, race, culture, heritage), isolation. Many countries have strong spirits of nationalism; fascism, Nazi, black power, white power, mother Russia, German pride, Irish pride, Slavic pride, Italian pride, and so on. Violence, terrorism, tribalism, ethnic purity, racism, prejudice.

NECROMANCY

Magic, black magic, witchcraft, voodoo, conjuration, divination, wizardry.

NERVOUSNESS

Tension, fear, anxiety, apprehension, restlessness, worry, distress, timidity.

NEST

Habitation, dwelling, hiding place, den of iniquity, breeding place. Command demons that are hiding in people to come out of their nests.

NET

Trap, snare, web, pitfall, gin, spider web (Isaiah 59:5), booby trap.

NETWORK

Organization, order, system, maze, tangle, plan, structure, chain (demons set up networks in regions and individuals).

NIGHTMARE

Monster, incubus, succubus, phantasm, fear of night, fear of the dark, fear of nightmares, *"terror by night"* (Psalm 91:5), bad dreams.

O

OBSCENITY

Vulgarity, indecency, filthiness, shamelessness, vileness, licentiousness, immorality, uncleanness, lust, perversion, pornography, bestiality, wantonness, profanity, lewdness, promiscuity.

OBSESSION

Domination, control, mania, passion, inordinate affection, preoccupation (with people, things, thoughts), fixation.

OBSTRUCTION

Obstacle, hindrance, blockage, barrier, resistance, difficulty, block (many spirits of blockage and obstruction including choking, closed doors, cut off, cut off at the source, gag, muzzle, shackle, bind, check, halt, bring to a standstill, and so on).

OCCULT

Secretive, hidden, mysterious. Includes witchcraft, sorcery, divination, ESP, hypnosis, fortune-telling, crystal ball, Ouija board, tarot cards, Freemasonry, martial arts, magic, séances, clairvoyance, mediums, psychics, readers, advisors, necromancy, handwriting analysis, astrology, yoga, metaphysical healing groups, hypnotism, occult movies, occult programs, occult books, occult games, New Age movement, amulets, talismans, ankhs, yin yang, Eastern religions, transcendental meditation, familiar spirits, occult bondage, occult inheritance (opens the door for multiple curses of sickness, death, destruction, confusion), channeling, Santeria, Dungeons and Dragons.

OCTOPUS

Mind control, mind binding, mental torment, migraine, headaches, octopus (spirits with tentacles).

OPPRESSION

Heaviness, iron hand, iron fist, heavy hand, pressure, strain, burdens, heavy load, weights, torment, affliction.

ORION

A great hunter, a mighty hunter, nimrod, pride, name meaning "blooming," "beautiful," "strong"; confidence, impiety. (See Job 9:9.)

ORTHODOXY

Conservatism, ultra-conservatism, fundamentalism, religious spirits, resistant to change, strictness, rigidness, inflexibility, unbending, unyielding, dogmatic, tradition.

OSTRICH

Sticking one's head in the sand. Hiding, withdrawal, fear, hardness of heart, lack of wisdom (Job 39:13–17), run and hide, escape.

OUTCAST

Rejection, castaway, Ishmael, exile, vagabond, wanderer, rover, leper.

OWLS

Idolatry, creatures of the night. (Ceramic owls and frogs have been known to attract demons into houses.)

P

PAIN

Tormenting spirits of pain including head-aches, migraines, mental pain (caused by octopus spirit of mind control), stomach pain, arthritis, rheumatism, back pain, neck pain. Pain spirits can operate throughout the body, loins (Isaiah 21:3). Perpetual (Jeremiah 15:18), affliction (Psalm 25:18), hurt, painful memories, emotional pain.

PALMISTRY

Palm reading, fortune-telling, divination, occult.

PALSY

Paralysis, atrophy, cerebral palsy, spirits operating in and controlling the spine.

PANTHER

Black cat, wild cat, tiger; wild, savage, fierce, ferocious, violent.

PARADOX

Confusion, maze, puzzle, dilemma, perplexity.

PARALYSIS

Very powerful spirit controlling the spine; disability, stroke, palsy, atrophy, depression, sadness, suicide, hopelessness, despair, crippling, paraplegic, lameness.

PARANOIA

Fears, madness, mental illness, suspicion, mistrust, distrust, apprehensiveness, persecution, jealousy, envy, confrontation.

PARASITE

Leech, sponge, begging, moocher, bloodsucker, dependency, control, manipulation.

PASSION

Rage, blind rage, temper, fit, anger, fury, vehemence, lust.

PASSIVITY

Listlessness, heaviness, slumber, stoicism, laissez-faire, laziness, slothfulness, mental dullness, lukewarmness, idleness, disinterest, funk, indifference, lethargy, withdrawal, escape, Ahab.

PERDITION

Damnation, ruin, destruction, hell, abyss, reprobate, desolation.

PERFECTIONISM

Pride, vanity, ego, frustration, criticism, judgment, irritability, intolerance, rigidity, exactness, fussiness, overcritical, schizophrenia, anger.

PERPLEXITY

Confusion, paradox, maze, puzzle, bafflement.

PERSECUTION

Unfairness, fear of judgment, condemnation, accusation, rejection, paranoia, sensitiveness.

PERSISTENCE

Linger, last, endure, continue. Conditions and problems that persist after prayer, Bible reading, praise, and so on are usually the result of curses and demons.

PERVERSION

Perverse (Isaiah 19:14), crooked, deviation, misuse, sexual perversion, homosexuality, lesbianism, incest, religious perversion, false doctrine, heresy, witchcraft, pride, vanity, lust.

PESSIMISM

Cynicism, doubt, unbelief, suspicion, hopelessness, discouragement, distrust, doom and gloom.

PHANTOM

Incubus, succubus, nightmare, delusion.

PHOBIA

All kinds; fear, irrational fear, horror, fright, panic, dread, apprehension.

PIG

Gluttony, greed, self-indulgence, uncleanness, hog.

POISON

Venom, snakebite, gall, wormwood, bitterness, unforgiveness, false teaching, false doctrine, heresy, toxic (friendships, relationships), malignant, ruinous, spite, slander, hurt.

POMPOUS

Pride, arrogance, self-importance, haughtiness, self-exaltation, grand, showy, boasting, vanity, airs, pretence, self-applause, high-and-mighty, puffed up, stuck-up, uppity, overbearing.

PORNOGRAPHY

Erotica, hard-core, X-rated (books, movies, videos), peep shows, obscenity, fantasy, lust, perversion (oral sex, anal sex, homosexuality, lesbianism, orgies, bisexuality), mind control, lewdness, lasciviousness (1 Peter 4:3), uncleanness (Ephesians 5:3), sensuality, carnality, whoredom, prostitution, voyeurism, lust of the eyes, masturbation, nudity, a marriage-breaking spirit, curiosity, shame, guilt, condemnation, sexual impurity, defilement.

PREEMINENCE

Pride, self-exaltation, Diotrophes (3 John 9), superiority, dominance, control, competition, evil ambition, jealousy, envy, importance, prestige, rivalry.

PREJUDICE

Bigotry, anti-Semitism, anti-Americanism, hatred of black people, hatred of white people, apartheid, white power, black power, racism, intolerance, bitterness, anger, accusation, bias, Jim Crow, narrow-mindedness, ignorance, pride of race, premature judgment, religious prejudice, cultural prejudice, racial prejudice, rejection, self-rejection, fear.

PERSECUTION

Unfairness, fear of judgment, fear of condemnation, fear of accusation, fear of reproof, sensitiveness.

POSSESSIVENESS

Control, covetousness, schizophrenia, greed, envy, jealousy, insecurity, rejection.

PRIDE

Leviathan (Job 41), arrogance, little pride ("Everybody has me"), hidden pride, hardness of heart, stubbornness, rebellion, rejection, anger, rage, pride of (knowledge, success, color, race, position, power, culture, religion, family name), vanity, ego, self-righteousness, haughtiness, importance, judging, arrogance, self-importance, self-conceit, self-love, self-exaltation, superiority.

PROFANITY

Cursing, blasphemy, filthy conversation, perverse speech, pride, railing, obscenity, impiety, irreverence, anger, bitterness, hatred.

PROMISCUITY

Harlotry, whoredom (Hosea 5:4), sexual impurity, lewdness, looseness, lust, perversion, adultery, fornication, uncleanness, wild, wanton.

PROSTITUTION

Paphian, Aphrodite, whoredom, harlotry, Jezebel, pimping, abuse. Comes in through a curse, rape, and sexual abuse. Rejection, rebellion, hurt, drugs, alcohol.

PSYCHIATRY

Psychology, spirits of Sigmund Freud, mind control, confusion.

PSYCHIC

Psychic spirits of inheritance, ESP, spiritualism, clairvoyant, reader, adviser, occult.

PYTHON

Divination (Acts 16:16–18). A large constrictor. (These spirits squeeze the life out of relationships, churches, and so on.)

Q

QUICK-TEMPERED

Temper, anger, rage, bitterness, sensitivity, fighting.

R

RACHEL

Refusing comfort, grief (Matthew 2:18). Works with abortion aftermath.

RAGE

Fury, anger, murder, wrath, passion, raving, blind rage, burning rage.

RAHAB

Pride, a sea monster, name meaning "outrageous," "violent," "tumult," "fierce," "proud," "vain," "insolent" (Psalm 89:10; Isaiah 51:9).

RAPE

Assault, abuse, molestation, ravishment (Lamentations 5:11), defilement, hurt, bitterness, anger, murder, revenge, retaliation, hatred (of men or abuser), fear (of being raped or abused), torment, confusion, guilt, shame, memory recall, trauma, shock, abortion, suicide, insanity, breakdown. Opens the door for spirits of harlotry, prostitution, frigidity, and whoredom to enter.

RATIONALIZATION

Intellectualism, logic, analytical (hard time receiving the things of the Spirit), mind idolatry.

REBELLION

Anti-submissiveness, self-will, selfishness, self-deception, self-delusion, self-seduction, accusation, judgmental, pride, unteachable, suspicion, distrust, persecution, confrontation, control, possessiveness, disobedience, stubbornness, witchcraft (1 Samuel 15:23), sedition, defiance, hatred of authority, anger, hatred, violence, murder, resentment, unforgiveness, retaliation, memory recall, paranoia, bitterness (root of), hurt, rejection (opens the door for rebellion), nonconformity.

REJECTION

From mother, father, siblings; self-rejection; rejection from the womb. Hurt, deep hurt, wounded, bruised, low self-esteem, anger, bitterness, unforgiveness, lust (a substitute for true love), fantasy lust, harlotry, pride (a compensating spirit for rejection), envy, jealousy, inferiority, insecurity, inadequacy, sadness, grief, sorrow, self-accusation, self-condemnation, depression, hopelessness, despair, despondency, striving, achievement, performance, competition, withdrawal, loneliness, independence, isolation, selfishness, criticism, covetousness, self-pity, possessiveness, perfectionism, outcast, castaway, black sheep.

Rejection can open the door for a multitude of spirits, including rebellion, pride, bitterness, self-pity, escape, guilt, inferiority, insecurity, fear, hopelessness, fear of judgment, defensiveness, distrust, discouragement, disrespect, hardness, perfectionism, false compassion, false responsibility, material lust, sexual lust, perverseness, self-accusation, compulsive confession, self-promotion, attention-getting, control, withdrawn, fear of love, self-deception, suicide, unworthiness, shame, vanity, intolerance, frustration, impatience, unfairness, pouting, unreality, daydreaming, vivid imagination, self-awareness, timidity, shyness, sensitiveness, talkativeness, nervousness, tension, inordinate affection for animals.

RELAPSE

Backsliding, lapse, regression, setback, apostasy, reversion, reversal, the skids, return, falling back.

RELIGIOUS

Doctrinal obsession, denominationalism, legalism, conservatism, intolerance, dogmatic, tradition, religious prejudice, division, deception, control, mysticism, religious pride, imbalance, idolatry, sectarianism, heresy, false doctrine, error, confusion, unbelief, resistance to the truth, argumentativeness, cults (Jehovah's Witnesses, Christian Science, Mormonism, Theosophy, Scientology, Spiritualism, Eastern religions, Hinduism, Islam, Bahaism, Unity, Freemasonry).

Hypocrisy, Pharisee, one true truth (Church of Christ), self-righteousness, holier-than-thou, false holiness, false tongues, false prophets, salvation by works, metaphysics, wolf, hireling, bondage, another Jesus, another spirit, another gospel, angel of light, philosophy, itching ears, seducing spirits, doctrines of devils, orthodox (Greek, Russian, Eastern), icons.

Praying to the saints, false baptism, salvation by baptism, rigid, strict, stern, exact, over-religious, guilt, condemnation, schismatic, apostasy, bigotry, fanaticism, papism, popery, eminence, preeminence, ceremonies, rites, Mariolatry, relics, backsliding, skepticism, materialism, superstition, ceremonial, false priesthood, fear of losing salvation, fear of backsliding, formalism, fear of God, fear of hell, religiosity, judgment, seduction, intolerance.

RESENTMENT

Bitterness, spite, revenge, retaliation, cruelty, anger, hatred, unforgiveness, offense, gall, wormwood, disgust, rage, murder, malice, jealousy, envy, suspicion, animosity, irritation, annoyance, indignation.

RESISTANCE

To the truth, the Word, the Holy Spirit, salvation, deliverance, praise and worship, and prayer. Opposition, stubbornness, hardness of heart, obstinate, impediment, obstruction, fighting, arguing, debate, fear, hatred of the truth, hatred of God, Jannes and Jambres (2 Timothy 3:8), rebellion, disobedience, contention, witchcraft, unbelief.

RESTLESSNESS

Insomnia, roving, nervousness, worry, anxiety, tension, impatience.

RETARDATION

Impediment, handicap, hindrance, obstruction.

RETALIATION

Revenge, spite, bitterness, murder, self-vindication, eye for an eye, tooth for a tooth, counterattack, reprisal, satisfaction, anger, wrath, malice, rage.

REVENGE

Spite, ill will, bitterness, animosity, venom, fury, wrath, violence, cruelty, eye for an eye, tooth for a tooth, vendetta, counterattack, malice, hurt, rejection, wounded spirit.

RIGID

Stiff, hard, inflexible, unyielding, firm, set in your ways, stubbornness, strict, narrow-minded, prejudice, ironclad, harshness, resistance to change.

RUDENESS

Disrespect, pride, arrogance, sharpness, ignorance, harshness.

RUTHLESSNESS

Merciless, heartless, hardness of heart, unforgiveness, cruelty, cold-blooded, cutthroat, sternness, pitiless, harshness, pride, arrogance, tyrant, behemoth (Job

40:15–24), control, domination, selfishness, viciousness, without feeling, bitterness, spite.

S

SABOTAGE

Treachery, subversion, treason, mischief, hurt, rebellion.

SACRILEGIOUS

Profanity, obscenity, irreverence, heresy, infidel, impious, unholy, corruption, indecent.

SANCTIMONIOUS

Self-righteousness, holier-than-thou, Pharisee, false piety, false holiness, hypocrisy.

SATAN

Lucifer, Beelzebub, Belial, Molech, Abaddon, Apollyon, Azazel, Evil One, Wicked One, Serpent, Dragon, Red Dragon, Prince of Darkness, the Adversary, Archdemon, Asmodeus, Liar, Murderer, god of this world.

SATYR

Goat, Libertine, debaucher, playboy, fornicator, seducer, Don Juan, stud, lady-killer, womanizer, Casanova, rapist, bed-hopper, gigolo.

SCAPEGOAT

Victim, laughingstock, target, whipping boy.

SCHISM

Division, sectarian, faction, heresy, contention, strife, denominational spirits, variance, pride, carnality.

SCHIZOPHRENIA

Double-mindedness, instability, confusion (James 1:8), rooted in rejection. The schizophrenic's personality (the real personality) has never developed, due to demonic interference. The demonic personalities of Rejection (inward) and Rebellion (outward) have taken over, causing a split personality.

Spirits operating under Rejection include lust, fantasy, perverseness, suicide, guilt, pride, vanity, loneliness, fears, attention-seeking, inferiority, withdrawal, sensitivity, frustration, impatience, inordinate affection for animals, self-rejection, envy, despondency, despair, discouragement, hopelessness, unworthiness, and shame.

Spirits operating under Rebellion include accusation, selfishness, pride, hatred, resentment, violence, disobedience, suspicion, distrust, persecution, self-will, stubbornness, bitterness, anger, unteachableness, control, witchcraft, possessiveness, unforgiveness, retaliation, self-deception. (See *Proper Names of Demons* by Win Worley. Also see *Pigs in the Parlor* by Frank Hammond.)

SCORPION

Torment; spirits of fear, death, poison, pain (Luke 10:19).

SÉANCE

Endor (1 Samuel 28:7). Divination, witchcraft, necromancy, conjuration, medium, familiar spirits, apparitions, ghosts, phantoms, occult.

SEA SERPENT

Leviathan, Rahab, dragon.

SECT

Division, pride, schism, carnality, false teaching, denominations, separation, cults, contention, Pharisee, Sadducee, bigotry, dogmatic, error, heresy, control.

SEDUCTION

Jezebel, Delilah.

SELFISHNESS

Self-love, self-indulgence, egotism, narcissism, covetousness, stinginess, rejection.

SELF-LIFE

Self-love, self-pity, self-destruction, self-rejection, self-hatred, self-righteousness, self-exaltation, self-promotion, self-will, self-indulgence, self-gratification, self-rule, self-esteem, self-made, self-deception, self-delusion, self-sufficiency, self-reliance, self-consciousness, self-centered, self-torture, selfishness, self-important, self-seeking, self-denial (me, myself, and I), vanity, ego.

SELF-WILL

Rebellion, stubbornness, disobedience, anti-submissiveness, egotism.

SENSITIVENESS

Self-awareness, fear of man, fear of disapproval, retaliation, oversensitiveness, hypersensitivity, touchiness, quick-tempered, easily hurt, rejection, deep hurt, anger, bitterness, impatience, excitability, susceptibility (to witchcraft, mind control, hurt, lust, pride), irascibility.

SENSUALITY

Pleasure, love of pleasure, epicurean, gluttony, drunkenness.

SERPENT

Python, constrictor, cobra, asp (Romans 3:13), viper, sea serpent, Leviathan, lust, deception, subtlety (2 Corinthians 11:3), cunning, slyness. (See Luke 10:19.)

SEXUAL

Sexual impurity, Paphian, Aphrodite.

SHAME

Disgrace, dishonor, hurt, embarrassment, scandal, reproach, fear, guilt, condemnation.

SHYNESS

Rejection, self-consciousness, timidity, fear, hesitation, fear of rejection, withdrawal, apprehension, nervousness, bashfulness, low self-esteem.

SICKNESS

Infirmity (Luke 13:10–13), disease, malady, plague, cancer, arthritis (whole group of spirits under *itis,* which means "inflammation," including bronchitis, appendicitis, phlebitis, and so on), blood disease, bone disease, lung disease, heart disease, death, destruction, unforgiveness, bitterness, infection, virus, high blood pressure, sugar diabetes, infirmities of all kinds by name. Chronic sicknesses and diseases are usually the result of curses of infirmity, death, and destruction.

SIEGE

Blockade, cutting off at the source, shut in, surround, boxed in, cutting off supply lines, siege warfare, starvation, famine, hopelessness, discouragement, death, destruction, suicide, fear, confusion.

SLANDER

Defamation, character assassination, accusation, cursing, libel, false report, lying, accuser of the brethren, malice, spite, bitterness, anger, hatred, evil speaking.

SLAVERY

Bondage (Romans 8:15), servitude, captivity, subordination, control, domination, legalism, ignorance, fear, rejection, self-rejection, fear of rejection, hatred, bitterness, unforgiveness, destruction, self-destruction, poverty, lack, debt. (Break curses of slavery over African-Americans.) Hatred of white/black people, fear of white/black people, bitterness toward white/black people, slave-master, Ishmael (Galatians 4:22), rebellion, stubbornness, sorrow, sadness, despair, hopelessness, despondency, frustration, confusion, destruction of the family priesthood (curse on males), Ahab, Jezebel, rape, molestation, sexual impurity, abuse, vagabond, wandering, plantation, slave mentality, failure, racism, prejudice, isolation, rage, murder, addiction, alcoholism.

SLOTHFULNESS

Sloth, laziness, slumber, idleness, lethargy, passivity, heaviness, sluggard.

SODOM AND GOMORRAH

Perversion, homosexuality, burning, consuming with fire, secret intrigues, hidden wiles, covered conspiracy, overbearing, tyranny, oppression.

SOOTHSAYING

Python, divination, false prophecy, astrology, horoscopes, psychic.

SORCERY

Drugs (Greek word: *pharmakeia*), witch-craft, magic, occult, charms, incantation, hypnotism, trance, spells.

SORROW

Grief, sadness, hurt, anguish, weeping, crying, lamentation, heartache, brokenhearted, despair, discouragement, loneliness, hopelessness.

SOUL TIES

Ungodly soul ties, false friendship, witch-craft, control, manipulation, deception, self-deception, blindness (spiritual), false love (formed through fornication), adultery. Ungodly soul ties need to be broken and evil spirits need to be cast out.

SPENDTHRIFT

Wasting, squandering, addiction to spending money, mishandling money, debt, poverty.

SPIRITISM

Séance, spirit guide, necromancy.

SPITE

Malice, animosity, cruelty, slander, resentment, hatred, anger, bitterness, gall, wormwood, envy, jealousy, hurt, unforgiveness, rejection, abuse.

SQUID

Mind-control spirits with tentacles, causing confusion, mind binding, mind racing, mental pain, migraine, and mental torment.

STEALING

Kleptomania, theft, lying, covetousness, shoplifting, pickpocket.

STERILITY

Barrenness.

STIFF-NECKED

Stubbornness, obstinacy, rebellion, disobedience, pride, Leviathan (Job 41).

STINGINESS

Covetousness, miser, selfishness, grudging (2 Corinthians 9:7), cheap.

STOICISM

Apathy, unconcern, indifference, bound and blocked emotions, hurt, deep hurt, fear of showing emotion, hardness of heart, fear of giving and receiving love, inability to give and receive love.

STRESS

Tension, worry, anxiety, mental breakdown, nervous breakdown, stroke, strain.

STRIFE

Contention, arguing, fighting, confusion, envy (James 3:16), discord, anger, bitterness, unforgiveness, pride, competition, hatred.

STRONGHOLD

Fortress, castle, bulwark, rampart, fortification, tower, citadel, bastion, garrison, high things, pride, imaginations (2 Corinthians 10:4–5), arguments, reasonings, disobedience, rebellion.

STRONGMAN

Ruling spirit (Matthew 12:29); strongman of fear, rejection, rebellion, lust, infirmity, witchcraft, and so on.

SUFFOCATION

Choking, asphyxiation, death, strangulation, smothering.

SUICIDE

Self-destruction, depression, gloominess, discouragement, death, kamikaze, Russian roulette, murder, despondency, despair, hopelessness, death wish, insanity, madness, confusion, rejection.

SUPERSTITION

Witchcraft, delusion, deception, fear, omens, accidents, demons, ghosts, fear of witchcraft, paranoia, idolatry.

SUSPICION

Distrust, fear, paranoia, accusation, doubt, rejection, hurt.

T

TALEBEARING

Gossip, busybody, strife, slander, lying, envy, jealousy.

TALKATIVENESS

Schizophrenia, nervousness.

TAROT CARDS

Witchcraft, divination, occult.

TASKMASTER

Slave driver, tyrant, despot, oppressor, cruelty, abuse, control.

TEMPER

Anger, rage, fury, wrath, fit, gall, wormwood, passion, irritation, annoyance.

TENSION

Anxiety, stress, apprehension, fear, worry, fretfulness, heavy burdens, tiredness.

TERMINATION

Death, terminal illnesses, destruction, premature death, cancer.

THIRD EYE

Eye of Ra, witchcraft, second sight. A witchcraft spirit operating between the eyes in the forehead area.

TIGER

Violence, fierceness, fighting, savage, wild.

TIMIDITY

Shyness, fear, withdrawal, rejection, fear of rejection, apprehension.

TRAGEDY

Calamity, catastrophe, trauma, shock, death, destruction.

TRANSVESTITE

Perversion, deviant, homosexuality, confusion, rebellion, rejection.

TRAUMA

Shock, anguish, suffering, turmoil, accidents. (Traumatic experiences open the door for spirits to enter, including fears, hurt, and bitterness.)

TRAVAIL

Toil, hard labor, trouble, anguish, torment, pain, sorrow, failure, frustration, despair, despondency, distress, pain, agony.

TREACHERY

Absalom (2 Samuel 15), betrayal, cruelty, hatred, rebellion, pride, jealousy.

TROUBLE

Affliction, oppression, burdens, adversity, misfortune, suffering, distress, hard times, sorrow, grief, vexation.

TUMOR

Infirmity, cancer.

TYRANT

Dictator, control, domination, pride, behemoth (Job 40:15–24), overlord, slave driver, taskmaster.

U

UNBELIEF

Doubt, hardness of heart, rebellion, disobedience, fear, skepticism, distrust, agnosticism, faithless, perverse, suspicion.

UNCLEANNESS

Unclean (Luke 4:33), foul (Mark 9:25), impurity, sexual uncleanness, immorality, filthiness, lewdness.

UNFAIRNESS

Persecution, schizophrenia, rejection.

UNREALITY

Pretension, daydreaming, schizophrenia, withdrawal, fantasy, denial.

UNTEACHABLE

Pride, stubbornness, rebellion, schizophrenia.

UNWORTHINESS

Inferiority, worthlessness, rejection, guilt, shame, condemnation, schizophrenia.

V

VAGABOND

Wandering, roaming, nomad, vagrant, drifting, aimlessness, roving, poverty, rejection, outcast, gypsy.

VANITY

Pride, ego, conceit, self-love, narcissism, self-importance, rejection, peacock, vainglory.

VICTIM

Sufferer, pushover, scapegoat, doormat, abuse, rejection, prey, sitting duck.

VIOLENCE

Rage, anger, fury, revenge, retaliation, murder, rejection, hatred, cruelty.

VOODOO

Sorcery, witchcraft, hoodoo, jinx, hex, vex, spell, incantation, conjuration, occult, spiritism, fear of witchcraft.

W

WALLS

Divider, separation, isolation, partition (Ephesians 2:14), self-protection, self-preservation, fear of rejection, fear of hurt, introvert, withdrawal, pride, demonic walls of rejection, hurt, fear, and so on.

WANDERING

Wanderers (Jeremiah 48:12), roaming, homeless, rejection, outcast, poverty. This spirit enters through the curse of the vagabond (Psalm 109:10).

WARLOCK

Sorcerer, wizard, male witch, conjurer, magician, medicine man, soothsayer, necromancer, diviner.

WHOREDOM

Prostitution, lust, Jezebel, perversion, uncleanness, rejection, seduction, rape, molestation, pornography, uncleanness, carnality, nakedness, lasciviousness, homosexuality, lesbianism, sodomy, idolatry, adultery, fornication, Gomer (Hosea 1:2–3). (See Hosea 5:4.)

WILD

Ishmael (Genesis 16:11–12), rejection, anger, rebellion, untamed, violence, antisubmissiveness, defiance, fighting, argumentative, stubbornness, self-rejection, pride, unruly, disobedience.

WILL

Spirits that control the will include lust, rebellion, stubbornness, self-will, blocked and bound will, loss of willpower, no will to fight, resignation, hopelessness, despair, and suicide.

WITHDRAWAL

Escape, isolation, introvert, rejection, fear, discouragement, passivity, sleepiness, alcoholism, drug addiction, hopelessness, despair, daydreaming, fantasy.

WOLF

Werewolf, carnivorous, ravenous; wolf in sheep's clothing, false prophets, teachers, and so on; greed, covetousness.

WORLDLINESS

Spirit of the world (1 Corinthians 2:12), carnality, sensuality, greed, materialism, antichrist, unbelief, vanity, lust, pride, ambition.

WORRY

Anxiety, fear, dread, apprehension, timidity.

WRATH

Anger, resentment, rage, bitterness, revenge, retaliation, murder, unforgiveness, pride.

X

X-RATED

Pornography, lewdness, nakedness, lust, perversion, whoredom, uncleanness, sexual impurity, homosexuality, lesbianism, orgy, lasciviousness, filthiness, obscenity, rebellion, disobedience, mischief, prostitution.

Y

YOGA

Occult, witchcraft, mind control, meditation, Kundalini.

Demons Attacking the Physical Body

taken from
A Manual for the Deliverance Worker
by Frank Marzullo and Tom Snyder

Evil spirits often dwell in certain parts of the body.

Abdominal Area and Pelvis

Spirits causing malfunction and problems in the liver, spleen, intestines, pancreas, bladder, kidneys, urinary tract, small and large bowels, reproductive organs, including spirits of cancer in these organs.

Bones, Neck, Back & Joints

Spirits causing pain, crippling, sway back, curvature of the spine, rheumatoid arthritis, arthritis, bursitis, multiple sclerosis, spirits affecting the spinal cord, nervous system, back bone, vertebrae, bone marrow.

Chest Area

Spirits causing heart problems and lung problems, abnormal blood pressure, irregular heartbeat, enlarged heart, breast cancer, tumors, growths, cysts, emphysema, respiratory problems.

Ears

Spirits of deafness, ringing in the ears, earaches, ear infections, inner ear problems, Meniere's syndrome, loss of balance, confusion, spiritual deafness, spirits of error, lying spirits.

Eyes

Spirits causing blindness, cataracts, glaucoma, floaters, nearsightedness, farsightedness, lazy eye, crossed eyes, dry eyes, all other diseases and weaknesses of the eyes, lust of the eyes, pornography, evil eye, witchcraft.

Head

Spirits causing strokes, brain damage, cancer, tumor, cysts, blood clots, epilepsy, meningitis, Alzheimer's disease, psychoses of all kinds, schizophrenia, paranoia, phobias of all kinds, double-mindedness, retardation, senility, hallucinations, manias, madness, confusion, forgetfulness, frustration, procrastination, mind-binding, bondage, worry, fear, dread, anxiety, stress, pressure, occult spirits, spiritism, satanism, nightmares, migraines, headaches, mental torment, suicide.

Mouth

Spirits causing tooth decay, gum infection, cavities, bad bite, jaw locking, grinding of teeth, canker sores, lip sores, loss of taste, bad breath, pyorrhea, stuttering, dumbness, oral sex, serpent spirits, lying spirits, swearing, blasphemy, dirty stories, gossip, blabbermouth, addiction, alcohol, tobacco, gluttony.

Navel

Often an entry point for demons coming through the umbilical cord before birth, or at birth. Spirits of inheritance and ancestral bloodline curses and spirits. (See *Demons Defeated* by Bill Subritzky).

Nose

Spirits causing loss of smell, bloody nose, postnasal drip, sinusitis, polyps, breathing difficulties.

Spine

Many spirits lodge in the spine including scoliosis, crooked spine, curvature, Kundalini, witchcraft, infirmity, crippling, palsy.

Throat

Spirits causing colds, viruses, thyroid disorders, goiters, laryngitis, swollen glands, polyps, tonsillitis.

Other Areas

Spirits of lust and fear can lodge in the stomach area. Lust can also lodge in any part of the body that has been yielded to sexual sin (Romans 6:16) including masturbation (hands), oral sex (mouth and tongue), homosexuality (rectum), and pornography (eyes).

Spirits of lust also dwell in the genitals. Many spirits of infirmity lodge in the spine (Luke 13:11). Witchcraft can lodge in the hands (Micah 5:12); and addiction spirits often lodge in the stomach, mouth, throat, and tongue (taste buds).

About the Author

John Eckhardt is called to impart and activate the gifts of the Spirit in order to raise up strong ministries in the body of Christ. A gifted man with a true apostolic and prophetic call on his life, his desire is to infiltrate the world with the Word of God. He is dedicated to perfecting the saints and training ministers to fulfill the call of God on their lives. Along with his apostolic and pastoral responsibilities, John Eckhardt produces a daily radio broadcast and "Perfecting the Saints," a daily television program, and he ministers throughout the United States and overseas.

John Eckhardt resides in a suburb of Chicago with his lovely wife, Wanda, and their five children.

To order books and tapes by John Eckhardt, please write or call:

Crusaders I.M.P.A.C.T.
P.O. Box 492
Matteson, IL 60422
(708) 922-0983

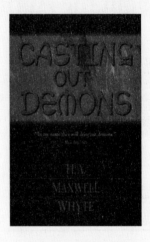

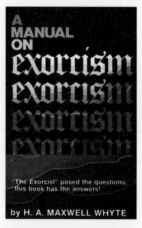

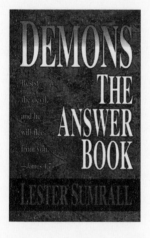

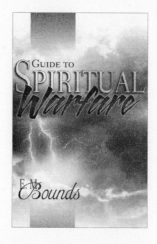

ANOTHER POWERFUL *Book*
from Whitaker House

Identifying and Breaking Curses
John Eckhardt

When you can identify curses by name, you can break them
by name. John Eckhardt discusses how you can identify
curses and break them, not only in your own life, but also
in the lives of others.

ISBN: 0-88368-615-5 • Trade • 64 pages